W9-AZG-647

Pebble® Plus

Creepy Crawlers

Centipedes

by Lisa J. Amstutz

Gail Saunders-Smith, PhD, Consulting Editor

Consultant: Wade Harrell
Vice President
American Tarantula Society

CAPSTONE PRESS
a capstone imprint

Pebble Plus is published by Capstone Press,
1710 Roe Crest Drive, North Mankato, Minnesota 56003.
www.capstonepub.com

Library of Congress Cataloging-in-Publication Data
Amstutz, Lisa J.
Centipedes / by Lisa J. Amstutz.
p. cm.—(Pebble Plus. Creepy Crawlers)
Summary: "Learn about centipedes, including how and where they live and how these creepy creatures are important parts of their world"—Provided by publisher.
Audience: 005-008.
Audience: K to grade 3.
Includes bibliographical references and index.
ISBN 978-1-4765-2053-7 (library binding)
ISBN 978-1-4765-3476-3 (eBook PDF)
1. Centipedes—Juvenile literature. I. Title.
QL449.5.A47 2014
595.6'2—dc23   2013008521

Editorial Credits
Jeni Wittrock, editor; Kyle Grenz, designer; Laura Manthe, production specialist

Photo Credits
Alamy: Bruce Coleman Inc./John Bell, 15, Papilio/Robert Pickett, 7; Corbis: Visuals Unlimited/Alex Wild, 19; Dreamstime: Ryan Pike, 1; Science Source: Francesco Tomasinelli, 17, Philippe Psaila, 13; Shutterstock: Henrik Larsson, 11, Konstantnin, 9, Marco Uliana, cover, RazvanZinica, 5, vlastas66, design element (throughout); Super Stock Inc.: Minden Pictures, 21

Note to Parents and Teachers

The Creepy Crawlers set supports national science standards related to life science. This book describes and illustrates centipedes. The images support early readers in understanding the text. The repetition of words and phrases helps early readers learn new words. This book also introduces early readers to subject-specific vocabulary words, which are defined in the Glossary section. Early readers may need assistance to read some words and to use the Table of Contents, Glossary, Read More, Internet Sites, and Index sections of the book.

Printed in China by Nordica.
0413/CA21300494
032013   007226NORDF13

Table of Contents

Lots of Legs

Look at all those legs! The word "centipede" means "100 feet." Not all centipedes have exactly 100 feet though. They can have anywhere from 30 to 300 feet.

5

Centipedes are arthropods.

Some are the size of a paperclip.

Others are as long as a ruler!

Centipedes live everywhere
except polar areas.

Home Sweet Home

Most centipedes stay in damp,
dark places so they don't dry out.
Their long, flat bodies slide easily
under rocks and logs.

Centipede Bodies

A centipede's body has many small parts, or segments. The parts bend so the centipede can move easily.

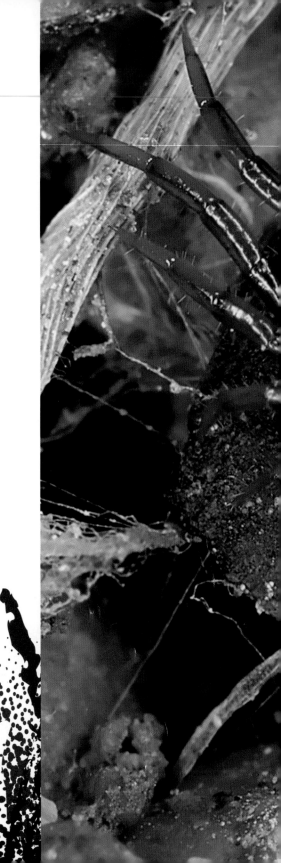

One pair of legs grows from each segment. Centipedes run fast to catch food or escape birds, toads, and other predators.

Night Hunters

When night falls, centipedes hunt.

Centipedes do not see well.

Their long antennae smell and

feel food nearby. Antennae also

sense danger.

Centipedes eat insects, worms, and other small animals. They bite their prey with fanglike claws filled with venom.

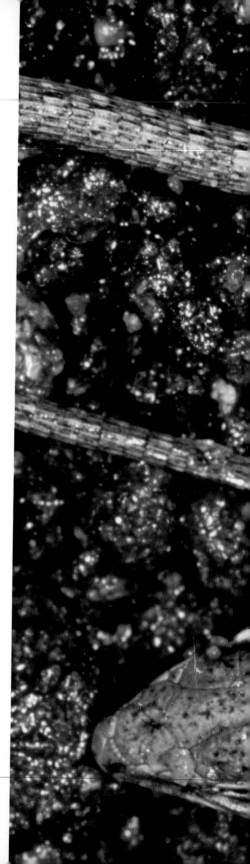

The Life of a Centipede

Female centipedes lay eggs.

Some baby centipedes, or nymphs, look like small adults.

Others have only eight legs.

They grow more when they molt.

It's best not to touch centipedes.

They may bite if they are scared.

But centipedes are fun to watch.

Their creepy, crawly bodies

are amazing!

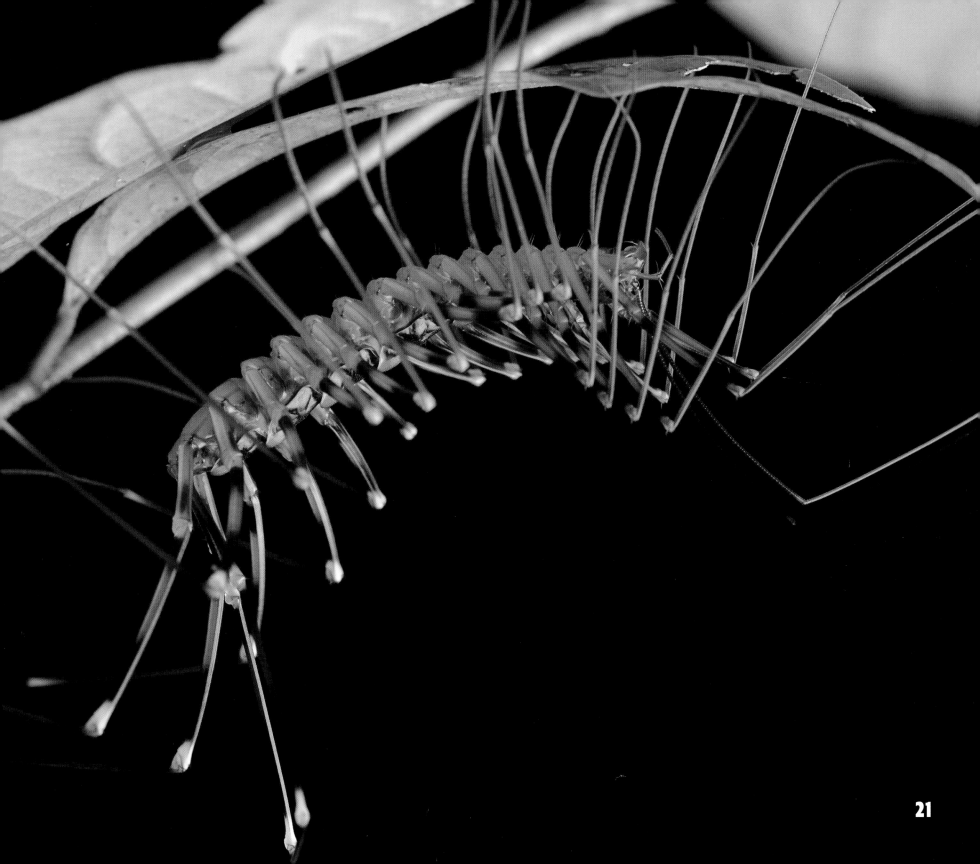

Glossary

antenna—a feeler on an animal's head

claw—a hard, curved nail on the foot of an animal

damp—slightly wet

fang—a clawlike tooth that squirts out venom

insect—a small animal with a hard outer shell, six legs, three body sections, and two antennae; most insects have wings

molt—to shed an outer layer of skin; after molting, a new covering grows

nymph—a young centipede; nymphs change into adults by shedding their skin many times

polar—having to do with the icy regions around the North or South Pole

predator—an animal that hunts other animals for food

prey—an animal hunted by another animal for food

segment—one of the ringed parts that make up a centipede's body

22

venom—liquid poison made by an animal to kill its prey

Read More

Bodden, Valerie. *Centipedes.* Creepy Creatures. Mankato, Minn.: Creative Education, 2011.

Lunis, Natalie. *Leggy Centipedes.* No Backbone! The World of Invertebrates. New York: Bearport Pub. Co., 2009.

Mitchell, Susan K. *Biggest vs. Smallest: Creepy, Crawly Creatures.* Biggest vs. Smallest Animals. Berkeley Heights, N.J.: Bailey Books/Enslow Publishers, 2011.

Internet Sites

FactHound offers a safe, fun way to find Internet sites related to this book. All of the sites on FactHound have been researched by our staff.

Here's all you do:

Visit *www.facthound.com*

Type in this code: 9781476520537

Check out projects, games and lots more at
www.capstonekids.com

Index

Word Count: 201
Grade: 1
Early-Intervention Level: 18